The
Brain Pioneer

The True Story of How
Barbara Arrowsmith-Young
Used Brain Science to Help
Children with Learning Disabilities

Written by Howard Eaton, Ed.M.
Illustrated by Kezzia Crossley

The author owes a great deal of gratitude to Arlene Prunkl, Chandra Wohleber, Claudia Kutchukian, Karen Orth, and Henriette Orth for their editing talents. The author is also deeply grateful to all the staff, students, and parents at Eaton Arrowsmith School for encouraging and supporting the completion of this book. The author also thanks Kezzia Crossley, Illustrator and Designer, for her amazing artistic talent and collaboration skills in creating the artwork for this book.

Glia Press Ltd.

Vancouver · Canada

Library of Congress Cataloging-in-Publication Data

Names: Eaton, Howard, author. | Crossley, Kezzia, illustrator

Title: The Brain Pioneer: the true story of how Barbara Arrowsmith-Young used brain science to help children with learning disabilities / written by Howard Eaton ; illustrated by Kezzia Crossley.

Description: Vancouver ; Canada : Glia Press Ltd., 2018.

ISBN XXX-X-XXXX-XXXX-X

Table of Contents

"It is through cognitive transformation that we help unlock each individual's gifts, allowing them to dare to dream."

Barbara Arrowsmith Young

Dedicated to all our pets who are our friends and healers.

Chapter 1
Early Life and Pioneer Ancestry

Barbara Arrowsmith-Young grew up in the 1950s and 1960s in Peterborough, Ontario. Barbara's parents, John and Mary, loved all five of their children.

John and Mary knew that hard work could overcome any obstacle. They would raise their children to have the same attitude toward life.

Barbara's dad, John, was a mathematician and a physicist. He worked as an electrical engineer and created over 30 inventions. He spent lots of time thinking about how to solve problems.

Barbara's mother, Mary, was a teacher, a nutritionist, and a school trustee. She spent many hours working in the Peterborough community to improve the school system. She was always busy, trying to make a positive difference in people's lives.

Barbara's school, Queen Mary Public School, was right across the street from her house. It was a red-brick building. Barbara's brothers, Alex, Greg, Donald, and William, did well at school. They loved making gadgets and building machines, just like their father.

Barbara was also expected to do well in school and make a positive contribution to society. At dinner, Barbara's dad would often ask the children, "What have you done today to make the world a better place?"

Barbara was sensitive, warm, and caring. Her middle name, Arrowsmith, was chosen by her parents as a reminder of her paternal grandmother, Louie May Arrowsmith.

Louie May was born in Provo, Utah, more than 130 years ago, in 1883. In 1891, when Louie May was eight, her family went on a one-year journey in a covered wagon: they were headed to Creston, British Columbia, to start a new life as farmers.

Louie May's family enjoyed reading. Her grandfather would read Shakespeare and the Bible each night around the fire during the one-year covered-wagon trek from Utah to British Columbia.

There was no school for Louie May to attend in Creston as the first school did not open until 1899, eight years after she arrived with her family. By then she was 16 years old. The first hospital in Creston did not open until 1930. Families like Louie May's were real pioneers.

Even without a formal education, Louie May continued to love reading and became the librarian in Creston.

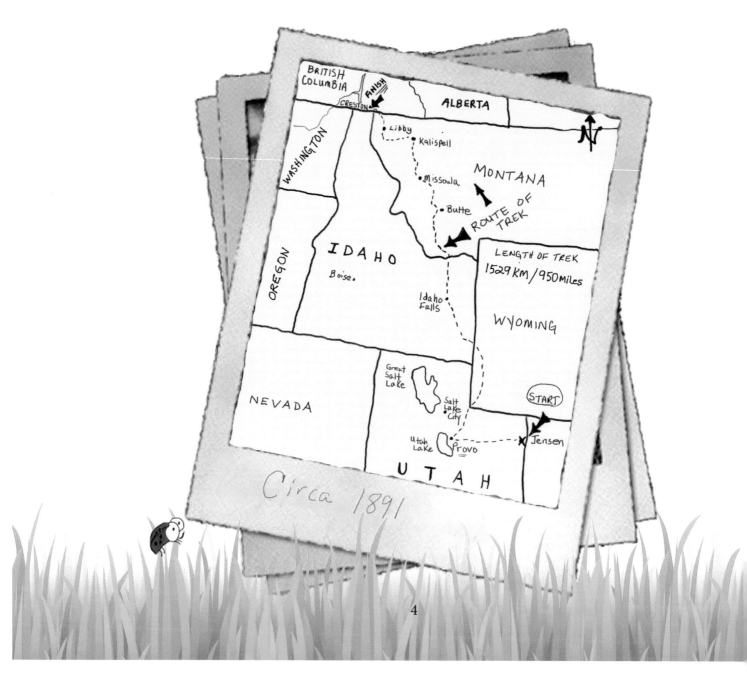

Barbara was born in Toronto in 1951, just a few years after the end of World War II. Although Toronto at that time was smaller than it is now with a population of just over a million, it was a much bigger and more bustling place than Creston, where her grandmother grew up. Barbara lived in Toronto for the first five years of her life before the family moved to Peterborough so her dad could work as an engineer at Canadian General Electric.

It did not take long for Barbara to show her own pioneering spirit, inherited from her grandmother Louie May. Like the pioneers, determination, inventiveness, passion, and persistence would define her character.

Barbara enjoyed playing outside with her brothers. They loved hide-and-seek, riding bikes, and, when their dad made a rink in their backyard, skating. Her father and mother noticed that Barbara was more accident-prone than her brothers. When she came in she often had bruises on her arms and legs from falling or from bumping into trees, bikes, and lawn furniture.

One day when she was three, one of her older brothers dared Barbara to jump over a Christmas tree her father had left in the backyard. She ran as fast as she could to leap over the tree, but she didn't make it over. She landed in the middle of the tree with her face covered in sharp pine needles. Her father had to pull them out, one by one.

There was also that time back when they still lived in Toronto and Barbara was playing in the driveway. She had invented a game called Matador and Bull. She decided she would be the bull, and the parked family car would be the matador. She charged the car with great excitement, ready to veer aside at the last moment like a real bull in a Spanish bullfight. That did not happen. She ran straight into the car at full speed! Instead of missing the car at the last minute, she ended up *in* the car with a towel on her head to stop the bleeding as her mother drove her to the hospital to get stitches. Barbara's mother wondered if her daughter would survive past age 5 as she was experiencing many more accidents than any of her brothers.

Chapter 2
Trouble at School

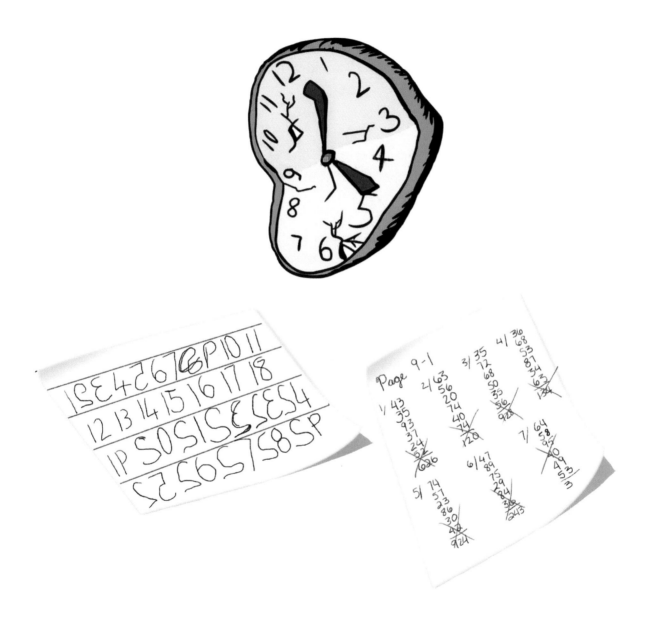

In first grade at Queen Mary Public School in Peterborough, Barbara wrote her letters and numbers backward. She also printed from right to left, not left to right. When she had to do printing, she got stressed out, which made her palms sweaty. The sweat on her palms then smudged her printing, making a mess, as she moved from right to left across her notebook. Her teachers were not happy with those backward letters and all the smudging, and they often made her redo her work. Barbara felt frustrated with printing, and later with cursive writing, too.

Then Barbara was put into the Turtle reading group at school! Her teacher had divided the students into three groups. The Squirrels were the fastest readers, and the Rabbits were the average readers. The Turtles were the slow readers. Tears streamed down her face: she wanted to be a Squirrel.

Math was also hard. Barbara could not understand how to add. She picked numbers at random and added them in a mixed-up way. Her answers were almost always wrong.

Barbara started putting up her hand in class to go to the washroom so she could escape reading or math. She would hide out for as long as she could (sometimes up to 45 minutes!) before returning to class.

Barbara began to despise school.

Barbara's parents and her teachers couldn't understand why she was struggling in school. If you sat down and had a chat with Barbara on the front porch of her Peterborough home you wouldn't have guessed she was so behind in school. She would have seemed much like anybody else her age, chattering about her family and pets.

Back in the 1950s there was no science to explain why some children didn't learn certain subjects as quickly as other students did. You were either smart, average, or not smart. Barbara's reading and writing difficulties would today be known as *dyslexia*.

Classrooms at that time had no tutors or aides trained to work with children who struggled in reading, writing, and math. Nobody was testing for dyslexia or learning disabilities. Parents had to find their own way to help their children, and John and Mary were determined to help their daughter as much as possible.

There were parent-teacher meetings with Barbara's first grade teacher. The teacher explained why Barbara was a slow learner by saying, "Barbara has a mental block, and she will never learn like the other children." Barbara happened to be attending this meeting. For years afterward, she thought she had an actual wooden cube in her head, and that was why school was hard.

School never got much easier for Barbara. It mostly became harder and harder. But one thing she was really good at was memorization. She memorized as much as she could in school. Her mother helped with this by creating flash cards for math questions. Barbara raced home (it was handy that her house was right across the street from school) at lunchtime to practice.

The flash cards had the question on one side and the answer on the back. Barbara realized that if she asked her mother to sit in front of a window, then when her mother held up a flash card, sunlight would flow through the card, showing Barbara the answer on the back. There was nothing at all wrong with Barbara's ability to solve some types of problems!

But it didn't take too long for her mother to figure out what Barbara was doing, and then she made sure to put her thumb over the answer to block out the light.

By third grade, Barbara was doing her best to stay away from school. On school-day mornings, she often told her mother she was feeling sick. Her mom would put a thermometer into her mouth, and then—quick—while her mother was doing something else, Barbara placed the thermometer on a light bulb. When her mom turned back to check on Barbara's temperature, it looked slightly high. Fearing her daughter was sick, Barbara's mom let her stay home from school.

Barbara found inventive ways to survive her school years!

Barbara really did have an extraordinary memory. She remembered almost everything she heard and saw, but she struggled to understand what she remembered. Each memory seemed unrelated to other memories or to other pieces of information. The world of connections and relationships was a mystery to Barbara.

Barbara would ask questions like:

"What does 'father's brother' mean, or 'mother's sister'?"

"Why can't I visit my brothers in the other classrooms whenever I want to?"

"What does the fraction 2/3 mean?"

"What is the difference between 'before' and 'after'?"

"What do those hands mean on that clock?"

"Why do the hands on a clock move?"

These were all *relationship* questions, and Barbara found the ideas, or concepts, involved in relationships confusing.

To get a feel for Barbara's problem, hold out your hand. Imagine your palm is an idea or concept—like a cat—and your fingers are the pieces of information needed to build that idea, to tell you, in this case, what a cat is. One finger tells you a cat is a small mammal, another that it is a carnivore, another that it has retractile claws, another that it has fur, etc. If this part of your brain is working properly, all these pieces of information come together so you can understand your world. If it does not work properly, as in Barbara's case, all these pieces of data remain separate and disconnected and the world is a very confusing and frightening place without meaning. Barbara struggled with understanding cause and effect, or why things happened, because she could not make these connections. Her world felt out of her control, and no matter how hard she tried to make sense of things, she was left confused and frustrated and unhappy. Think about living in a world where everything is uncertain, like walking on quicksand, where the ground constantly shifts under your feet.

As Barbara moved into fifth, sixth, seventh, and eighth grades, her difficulties with understanding relationships grew worse. She couldn't understand math problems. She couldn't see how characters in a book were related to each other. She sometimes even had trouble understanding her friends and why they acted in certain ways toward one another. She could not understand jokes and so felt left out of the fun. She felt lonely most of the time. She had a picture in her head of herself looking through a window at people enjoying themselves on the other side, having a good time, and she longed to join in but couldn't because it was all too confusing.

Barbara's father spent hours tutoring her in math, trying to show her how to understand the relationships in math problems. After her father tried to help her, Barbara went down to the basement laundry room and banged her head on the dryer. She hoped this might pound some sense into her head.

Nothing worked. The world was confusing for Barbara. She felt she was living in a fog, a world of uncertainty.

Years later, when she was an adult, Barbara visited her old home and saw that the dents from her head were still on the dryer!

Barbara worked even harder in high school, trying to understand her subjects. Compared to her friends, it took her longer to write, read, do assignments, study for tests, and complete exams.

She did okay when she could memorize facts, but when she had to learn concepts, and when she had to understand the relationships between ideas, she struggled.

Barbara's grades ranged from A to F. On a test that required memorization, she might get 90 percent—an A. But on tests that required her to fully understand relationships, to "get" how information was connected, she often failed. Fortunately, high school had a lot of exams that only required memorization of facts.

But mostly Barbara was miserable. The stress took a toll on her health, causing headaches, stomachaches, and frequent colds and infections. As her high school years went by, she spent hours on her bed in tears, talking to Star, the family cat, about how unhappy she was. Star was a huge comfort, cuddling up with her and purring, no matter how bad school was for Barbara.

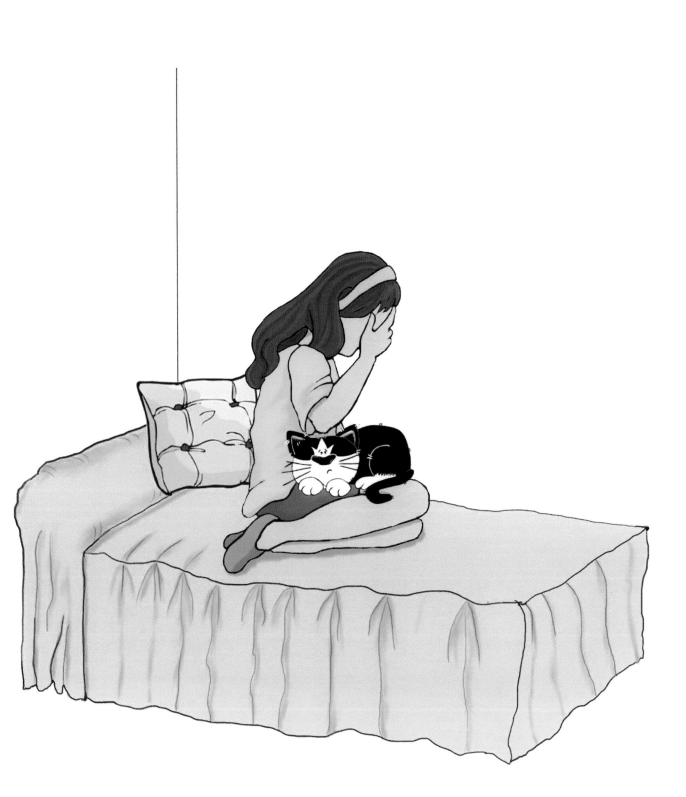

All children in the Young family were expected to go to university, and Barbara was no exception. She finished high school with a 70 percent average because of her amazing memory. In the early 1970s that was high enough for her to get into a good university.

Barbara was accepted at the University of Guelph. It was a two-hour drive from her family home in Peterborough. She started out studying nutrition, as her mother had. She had to take science courses to learn about food, digestion, health, and disease. But just like in high school, Barbara didn't do well in science courses because of her difficulty understanding the material she was studying.

After one year of studying nutrition, she decided to switch to child studies. She had enjoyed working with preschoolers at church in Peterborough. These courses involved a lot of memorization, so they were easy for Barbara.

Barbara was fascinated by children. At university, some of her courses required her to sit behind a one-way mirror and study children's behavior. Barbara's instructors told her she had a gift for understanding how and why children acted in certain ways through studying their nonverbal patterns of behavior and interactions.

Barbara realized that by studying child behavior she might finally be able to understand what was wrong with her. Why was school so difficult? Why did certain kinds of learning result in failure no matter how hard she tried?

Child Studies Department

For years Barbara had been trying to survive school without understanding what was wrong with her. She worked long hours, trying to memorize as much information as possible, but she still struggled to understand ideas and concepts and how they related to one another.

When Barbara started university in 1970, the field of learning disabilities was just beginning to develop in Canada. Learning disabilities were soon discussed at universities and schools across Canada and the United States.

Researchers found that learning disabilities existed even in children who were highly intelligent, or even gifted. In fact, to be diagnosed as having a learning disability, you had to have at least average intelligence. Children with learning disabilities can have strengths in certain areas of learning. Like Barbara, they might have trouble reading and writing but have an amazing memory. Barbara, in fact, had a photographic memory.

As the study of learning disabilities continued during the 1980s, governments and school systems decided that to help children with learning disabilities, schools needed to identify them through testing. Then they could provide those students with special education teachers and *compensations*, also known as *strategies*. Compensations were ways to work around their brain weaknesses. These weaknesses created lifelong learning problems, and research at the time had not identified any ways to actually *improve* or change the brain. Leaders in education felt the only way to help these students was to hire special education teachers to provide extra lessons to support those students in their regular academic classes.

During this same time, Barbara was studying in the field of learning disabilities, and she began to understand her own difficulties in school. She realized she had been using her own compensations and strategies to try to succeed at school. She used flash cards, reread her notes and textbooks, found quiet places to study with no distractions, and even spent entire nights in the university library, trying to memorize everything she needed to learn. This was her strength: memorization, and she used these strategies to make sure she memorized as much as she could in the time she was given.

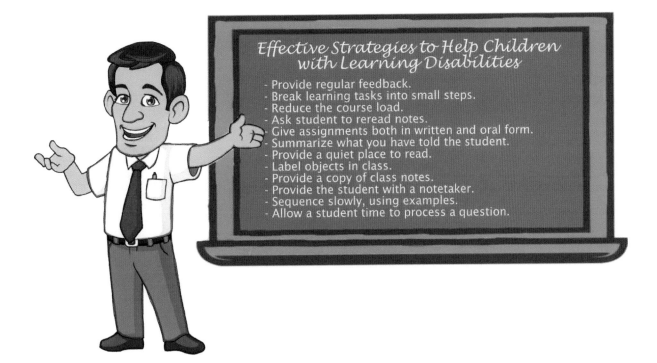

Effective Strategies to Help Children with Learning Disabilities
- Provide regular feedback.
- Break learning tasks into small steps.
- Reduce the course load.
- Ask student to reread notes.
- Give assignments both in written and oral form.
- Summarize what you have told the student.
- Provide a quiet place to read.
- Label objects in class.
- Provide a copy of class notes.
- Provide the student with a notetaker.
- Sequence slowly, using examples.
- Allow a student time to process a question.

When Barbara finished her child studies degree at the University of Guelph, she was hired by the university to work as the head teacher in a classroom used by researchers to study how children learned. This kind of research classroom is called a preschool labratory.

She was fascinated with why some children could not learn as well as others could. In this preschool laboratory, she tried to understand the behavior of the children based on Jean Piaget's work in child development. Piaget was the first psychologist to develop, in the 1930s, a theory of how children's cognitive functioning developed over time.

The Swiss-born Piaget believed that by watching children learn we can understand how they develop achievement skills such as math.

Barbara also observed children's social-emotional behaviors, which allowed her to see how children managed their emotions—such as frustration, anger, and happiness—when they engaged others in trying to build relationships.

Barbara carefully wrote down her observations of how children behaved while they interacted with tasks and with each other. She loved this work. This training gave her a remarkable skill base that she would use when building her own ideas on how to help children and adults with learning disabilities. She had found her true calling.

Jean Piaget 1896-1980

The Essential Piaget

The Construction of Reality in the Child

The Moral Judgment of the Child

The Child's Conception of Number

Chapter 3
Groundbreaking Research and Discoveries

Jean Piaget 1896-1980

Dr. Alexander Luria (1902-1977)

Dr. Mark Rosenzweig (1922-2009)

Barbara wanted to understand even more about how children learn, so she decided to go to graduate school in the fall of 1976 (this is when you want to keep studying after your four-year university degree). She was accepted at the University of Toronto's Ontario Institute for Studies in Education (also known as OISE). A degree in school psychology would allow her to work with children who had learning problems.

However, the stress of all the studying continued to wear down Barbara's body. Although she had found a subject she loved and could do well in, she still had to work extra hard. Her immune system (your immune system helps fight off illness) was functioning poorly as a result of stress, and she often got pneumonia, resulting in fevers, sweating, fatigue, and exhaustion. She realized that while she was determined to learn to help others with learning disabilities, her own learning was burning her out. She would get only four hours of sleep a night because of how hard she had to study every day, and even less sleep before an exam.

It took Barbara six years to complete her program (June 1982). Most students took only one or two years. She was able to get her course work done in two years; however, her thesis (a long essay on a specific subject that requires research) took another four years due to her learning disabilities.

Barbara's father had often told his children, "If you have a problem, find a solution." And that was exactly what Barbara did for her own learning disabilities.

In August 1977, Barbara came across a book by Dr. Alexander Luria (1902 -1977) called *The Man with a Shattered World* . Dr. Luria was a neuropsychologist from Russia. He was interested in how the brain works, and how different areas of the brain are in charge of specific behaviors. For example, understanding language and producing speech happen in specific areas of the brain called Wernicke's and Broca's area. The front parts of the brain (called the prefrontal cortex) are needed for paying attention and for making plans.

In his book, Dr. Luria described a young soldier who had served in the Russian army. In World War II, he suffered a traumatic brain injury. A bullet went into his brain and lodged in a specific section (called the parietal-temporal-occipital association area, or PTO). Although the bullet didn't kill the soldier, he was suddenly unable to do tasks he once found easy, such as reading a clock to tell the time, understanding fractions, or comprehending material in books or in conversations.

Dr. Alexander Luria (1902-1977)

PTO

As she read *The Man with a Shattered World*, Barbara realized that the problems the soldier experienced after the bullet lodged in his brain were the same ones she had been experiencing her entire life. After his traumatic brain injury, the soldier could not read a clock face to tell the time. He could not easily listen to someone and understand what they were saying, and as a result he often felt confused. He felt that he was living in a fog all the time. Those were the exact words Barbara used to describe how she felt.

But there was one major difference! *Barbara did not have a bullet in her brain.* Then why did she have the same problems? Clearly, the problem wasn't a wooden block, either. She began to wonder whether her brain worked differently from other people's brains, in a way that prevented her from making sense of the world. Maybe the way her brain was structured was causing her confusion and uncertainty.

The information in the book was Barbara's first step to actually finding a solution to her learning disabilities. Not just compensations and strategies, which work *around* a problem, but a solution to *overcome* the problem.

Barbara now knew that something was happening in her brain that could be causing her learning difficulties. Based on Dr. Luria's insight, she also knew which part of her brain was likely causing the difficulties. Dr. Luria wrote that the bullet had lodged in the left hemisphere of the soldier's brain, exactly where three brain regions connect to one another—the parietal-temporal-occipital association area. The parietal region is related to touch. The temporal region is responsible for sound and spoken language. The occipital region is responsible for sight.

This area of the brain, where these three brain regions connect, allows us to make sense of what we see, hear, and touch. If this area of the brain is not working well, understanding and connecting information will be very frustrating.

For example, seeing a dog in front of us, hearing the dog growling, and feeling its fur stand up under our fingers are all related to helping us understand that the dog is getting worried, afraid, or angry. Connecting all this information in our brain gives us meaning in this specific situation. If we can't connect this information, we may experience confusion as to what exactly is happening.

Barbara knew she was going to struggle for the rest of her life is she did not find a way to improve this area of her brain.

The Parietal-Temporal-Occipital (PTO) Association Area

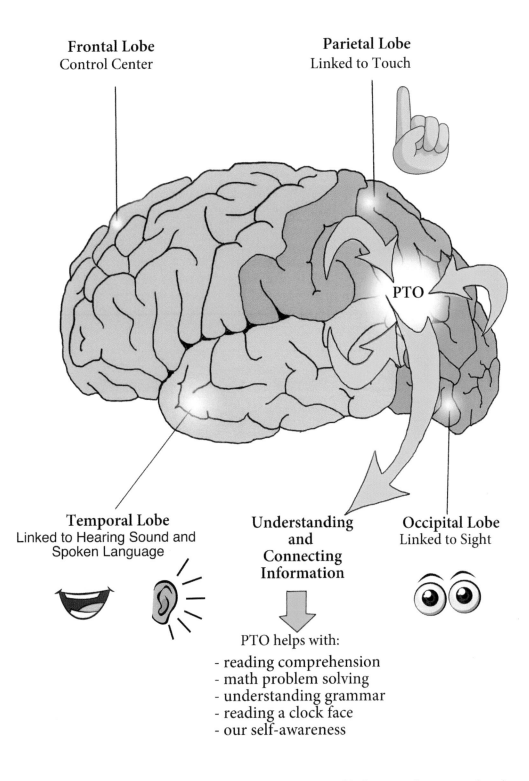

Frontal Lobe
Control Center

Parietal Lobe
Linked to Touch

PTO

Temporal Lobe
Linked to Hearing Sound and
Spoken Language

**Understanding
and
Connecting
Information**

Occipital Lobe
Linked to Sight

PTO helps with:

- reading comprehension
- math problem solving
- understanding grammar
- reading a clock face
- our self-awareness

Note: The lobes identified on the illustration above are responsible for many functions other than those described. For more information on the lobes, check out the Glossary at the back of the book.

41

A few months later, in October 1977, Barbara came across studies written by research psychologist Dr. Mark Rosenzweig and his colleagues. They were studying rats' brains at the University of California. Dr. Rosenzweig had discovered that if rats are given lots of toys, ladders, tunnels, and running wheels, over time their brains look much healthier than those of rats that are not given these things. Having an enriched environment full of opportunities for repetitive activities was good for stimulating rats' brains. In fact, the brains of rats that had more activities changed by growing in thickness and weight. They had more connections in their brains, which resulted in those rats being better at learning.

Barbara realized, from reading Dr. Rosenzweig's research, that the rats' brains were plastic (this means they can be molded—not that they are actually made out of the substance we know as "plastic"!); they were not hard-wired and fixed. They could be changed and shaped and molded as a result of experience.

Instead of their brains being like a lump of steel, they were more like the roots of a plant or tree. They could grow and become more complex if given the right environment.

This was an amazing discovery! Barbara thought that if a rat brain could change and improve, why couldn't a human brain? She just had to figure out a way to do this. Could she change her own brain? Could she find a way to make learning easier for herself?

Dr. Mark Rosenzweig (1922-2009)

Rat Brain Cell

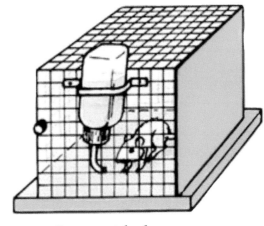

Impoverished
Environment

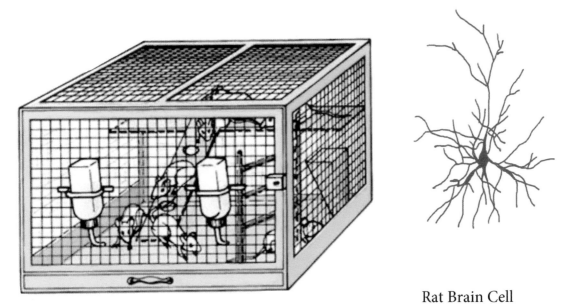

Enriched
Environment

Rat Brain Cell

Rosenzweig and Bennett (1972)

Barbara thought hard about these questions as she began to develop her own theory and solutions. What could she do to grow and improve her brain? Barbara knew that she had to make her brain understand relationships, so the idea of a clock face came to her mind. She could not tell time on a clock with hands (also known as an analog clock) without a lot of time and effort. The soldier in Dr. Luria's book had also had the same problem. They both had this problem because the area of their brains that reads a clock face (the parietal-temporal-occipital association area) was not functioning properly.

Barbara decided to practice telling time. If she did this over and over, like a rat repeating activities in an enriched environment, her brain might change. Could she stimulate this part of her brain?

She started by wearing multiple watches, both digital and analog, challenging herself to accurately tell the time on the analog watch and then checking the digital one to see if she was right. Then, in December 1977, now 26 years old, she drew clock faces on flash cards. Just like her mother had done with math flash cards, she wrote down hundreds of different clock faces on flash cards with the times written on the back. She practiced over and over, hours and days at a time.

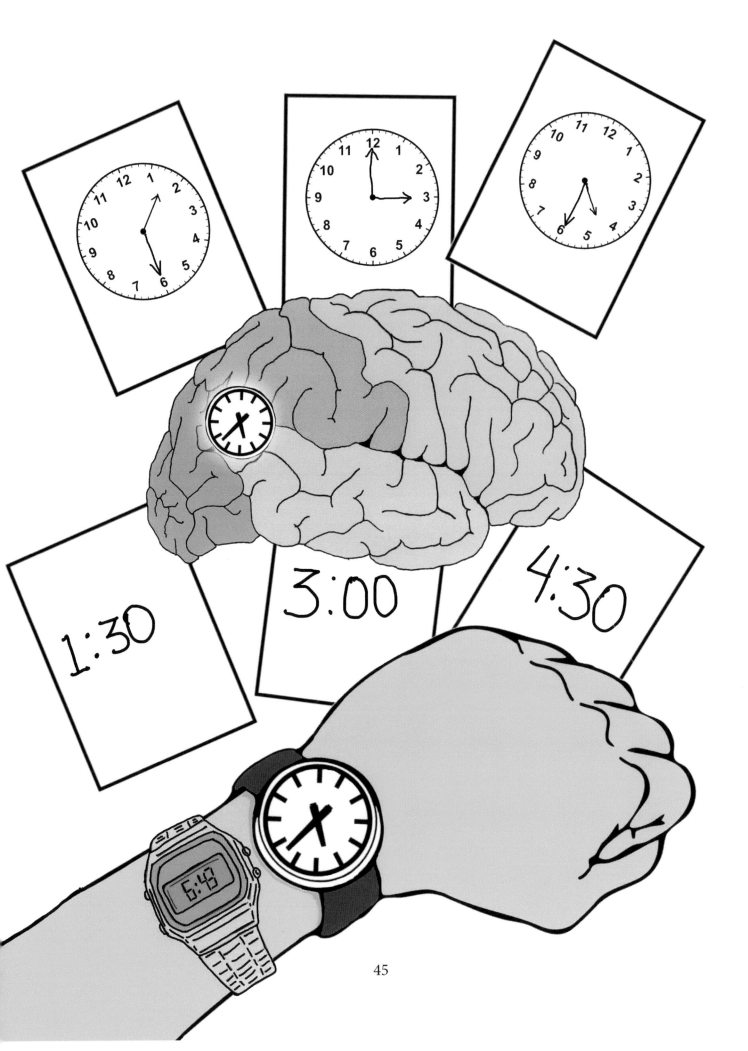

Barbara practiced every day for up to 12 hours a day. She wanted to not only read the clock face correctly, but also do it quickly. Speed and accuracy were important to Barbara. Weeks went by, and sure enough, slowly her brain began to change.

Barbara began noticing changes in other areas, too. She started being able to understand what she was reading without having to reread the material. Math concepts started to make sense. Her understanding of conversations she had with others began to improve. She could listen to people and feel certain she knew what they meant.

The part of the brain that helped her make sense of the world around her was changing. The neurons in that part of her brain were connecting, firing up, in ways that they could not before. It is important to note that neurons are special cells in our brain that communicate with one another so we can learn about and understand our world. These cells are the basic building blocks of all living things.

Now she was understanding connections and relationships in information that was presented to her, whether in books or in conversations with her friends and colleagues. She did not have to try to remember everything and then replay that information over and over to understand it. For the first time ever, Barbara felt she was living in real-time, where she could understand things as they happened, rather than living in lag-time, where she was always hours behind everyone else in understanding.

Barbara was thrilled! A rat brain could change—and a human brain could change as well.

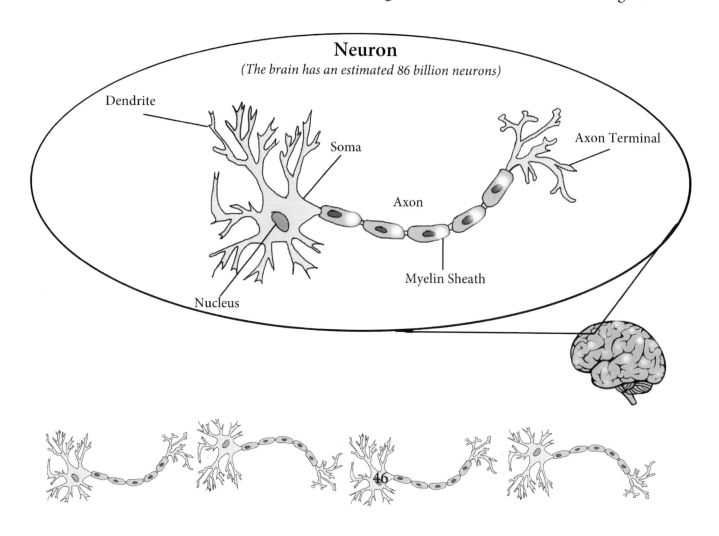

Neuron
(The brain has an estimated 86 billion neurons)

Dendrite

Soma

Axon Terminal

Axon

Myelin Sheath

Nucleus

Barbara had struggled since childhood with getting lost, even in familiar places, and not being able to read maps, sew from a pattern, or build a bookcase from a diagram (a spatial reasoning weakness). She was also accident-prone, often bumping into things (a kinesthetic perception weakness). After the matador-and-bull accident, her mother had said, "I'll be suprised if you live another year."

After experiencing success with her first exercise, Barbara created exercises for the areas of the brain responsible for spatial reasoning and kinesthetic perception. For example, she created an exercise that involved drawing shapes accurately with both eyes closed. With both eyes closed the brain must use other sensory feedback (not visual) to draw correctly. Over several months, she discovered that she was not getting lost while driving anymore, nor bumping into things.

Barbara was also finding that her thesis for graduate school was getting easier to complete. The brain exercises were having a positive impact on her academic work.

Barbara realized that more brain exercises could be created for learning difficulties, focusing on paying attention, planning, interpreting nonverbal information, remembering information, understanding language, memorizing visual objects, and understanding numbers.

Barbara was inspired by the thought of how she could help other children and adults with learning disabilities.

Chapter 4
A School of Her Own

Arrowsmith School

With the learning techniques she had created, Barbara decided to start the Arrowsmith School, named to honor the pioneering spirit she shared with her grandmother. She was 28 years old and still working on her master's degree. Her parents were very supportive of this idea and gave her a lot of encouragement.

In 1980, Barbara opened the doors to her school on Yorkville Avenue in Toronto, Ontario. Over the next 20 years, she created 19 different brain exercises for a variety of challenges faced by children and adults with learning disabilities. Her brother Donald was a big help in using technology to develop her ideas. Many of the exercises could now be delivered to the students by computer.

The school was like no other in the world. Its main goal was to help children with learning disabilities improve their brain functioning. It was not going to teach coping strategies, provide compensations, or provide tutoring to children who did not understand what they were learning.

Instead, the children would work on brain exercises created to target specific areas of their brains so they could learn independently. The school was designed to improve brain functioning and give children the freedom to succeed on their own at school. Barbara knew that learning disabilities did not have to be lifelong.

Over the years, Barbara's new school became a success.

Children in the Arrowsmith Program spend two to four years working on the brain exercises. Each week they improve their ability to think, plan, problem solve, retain information, interpret social situations, understand numbers, reason, and remember letter patterns needed for reading and writing. At the end of their time at Arrowsmith, they go back into a full-time regular education program. Often these children do not need special education classrooms, compensations, or other strategies to learn and progress in school.

Barbara has conducted research for more than 30 years. She has thousands of case studies of how individual students have improved their ability to learn. Scientists from universities in Canada and the United States are also studying children taking part in the Arrowsmith Program.

Neuroscientists today can use a magnetic field and pulses of radio wave energy to peek into the brain and see the impact of the brain exercises. They are looking deep into kids' brains using tools like functional magnetic resonance imaging (fMRI), myelin water imaging (MWI), and quantitative electroencephalography (qEEG). With these brain measurement technologies, they can see the brain changes in action!

These scientists are looking at children with learning disabilities after three months at Arrowsmith, and then after a year at Arrowsmith. They notice that their brains are changing.

Adults with traumatic brain injuries caused by car and motorcycle accidents, or with concussions from sports injuries or accidents such as falling off a ladder, are being studied as well. After just three months of the Arrowsmith Program, their brains are also showing improvement.

Before Program

3 Months after Program: increase in activity in prefrontal lobe

Functional Magnetic Resonance Imaging (fMRI)

Chapter 5
Into the Future

The idea that our brains can change is now accepted by top neuroscientists at universities around the world. The term used for that change is *neuroplasticity*, or *brain plasticity*. When plastic is soft it can be molded or shaped into a wide range of objects. In the same way, our brain can also be molded or shaped based on our experiences in life. Thus, the term *brain plasticity* is used to describe the potential of our brain to change over our lifetime.

Barbara has proven that challenging mental tasks you do regularly over a long period of time, with lots of repetition and increasing levels of difficulty, will change your brain. Whether that means learning to juggle, kick a soccer ball, remember a song or long lines of poetry, meditate, develop handwriting, play a musical instrument, or learn another language, your brain will change because of this kind of practice. Your brain is plastic. Your brain can grow, change, improve.

Like her grandmother Louie May Arrowsmith, Barbara is a pioneer. The trail ahead was no less challenging for Barbara than it must have been for Louie May and her family in the late 1800s. Barbara has faced many obstacles, including some educators, academics, and psychologists who believe that learning disabilities cannot be overcome.

Not everyone likes new ideas or is willing to accept them right away. A new idea can go against strong and powerful current ways of thinking that people have grown up with or studied for a long time. As a result, a group of people become very committed to believing in this way of thinking (called a *paradigm*). To change a paradigm (known as *paradigm change*) takes time, determination, passion, and resilience—and an open mind willing to consider observations that go against a current paradigm, and that are noteworthy and remarkable. Barbara has these characteristics in abundance.

Today, the Arrowsmith Program is used around the world. Schools in Canada, Australia, New Zealand, the United States, Malaysia, South Korea, Thailand, and Spain are using the program to help children and adults with learning disabilities.

After starting with her small school in Toronto, Canada, in 1980, with only a dozen students, Barbara Arrowsmith-Young is now an international educator helping thousands of children each day. Her book, *The Woman Who Changed Her Brain,* written in 2012, is an international bestseller and has been translated into Korean, Chinese, Polish, Japanese, and Spanish.

From that young girl who hid in the washroom at Queen Mary Public School to avoid reading and math, Barbara has come a long way. She is proof that if you put your mind to it, as her parents told her, you can find solutions to any problem!

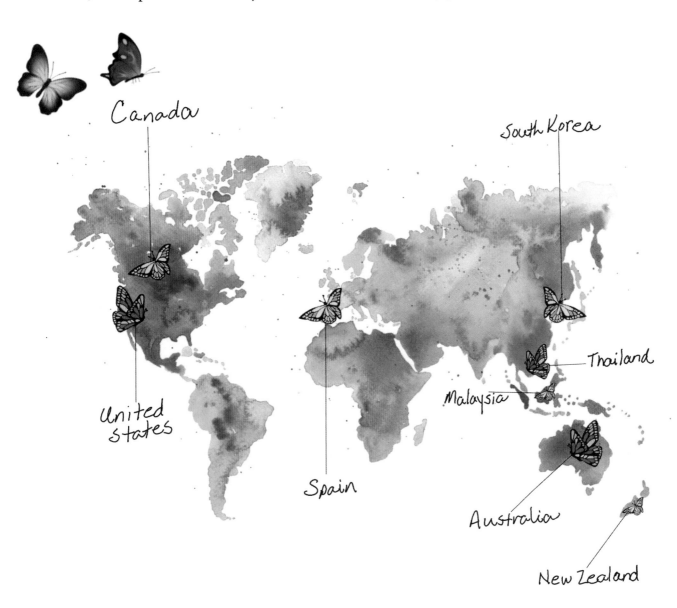

The History of Brain Plasticity Is a Scientific Revolution

If you want to be a scientist, it's important to understand how science changes over time. As scientific discoveries are made, they affect how people view the world around them. The big changes in science could be called revolutions. A revolution, in this context, is when there's a major change to an idea previously held up as indisputable fact.

An example of a scientific revolution would be the idea that the Earth is not the center of the universe. In the 1500s and 1600s, Nicolaus Copernicus, Johannes Kepler, and Galileo Galilei stated that this long-held belief was not true, and in fact it was the sun that was at the center of our solar system: the Earth revolved around the sun, rather than the sun around the Earth. This revolutionary idea (for which there was proof based on observation using new, more powerful telescopes for viewing the sky) was challenged by those who did not want to believe it in spite of the evidence. Galileo was even put under house arrest for proposing and teaching this theory!

A book about how scientific revolutions take place was written in 1962 by the American philosopher Thomas S. Kuhn. It is called The Structure of Scientific Revolutions. The main idea of the book is that new paradigms can take many decades to be understood, studied by researchers, and accepted by the scientific community. In scientific revolutions, when one group of scientists is holding on to an old idea but another is putting forth a new idea, a paradigm shift is happening.

Who can benefit from the revolutionary new discovery detailed in this book? Can children and adults with learning disabilities benefit? Barbara Arrowsmith-Young felt that they could. She started to experiment on herself in the late 1970s using clock drawings to improve her reasoning capacity. Over four decades later, she is now recognized as one of the first educators to show that knowledge of brain plasticity is important in understanding how we can improve educational outcomes for children with learning disabilities. In the 1970s and 1980s, this was a revolutionary idea in education, one that is now widely accepted.

In fact, scientists and academics began to wonder if the brain was plastic over 200 years ago. The first mention of brain plasticity was in connection with animals, and occurred in 1783. Michele Vincenzo Malacarne, an Italian surgeon and anatomist, discovered that trained dogs and birds had more folds in their cerebellums than untrained ones. He was surely suprised by this. What he was observing was brain plasticity at work. The more an animal interacts in a physically enriched environment, the more its brain grows. Folds on the surface of the brain provide more surface area for processing information.

In the 1800s other scientists started talking about the fact that the brain is likely able to change due to experience. These scientists included Eugenio Tanzi, an Italian psychiatrist and professor of psychiatry in Florence; Ernesto Lugaro, also an Italian psychiatrist, who worked at the Psychiatric Hospital of San Salvi in Florence; William James, a famous American psychologist and philosopher at Harvard University; and Santiago Ramon y Cajal, a Spanish physician and pathologist. In their writings, these scientists discussed how the brain could be influenced by our experiences and behavioral habits.

Ernesto Lugari first introduced the term plasticity into the neurosciences in 1906. Over 40 years later, in 1948, Jerzy Konorski, a Polish neurophysiologist, used the term neural plasticity in a book he had written. At almost the same time, Donald O. Hebb, a psychologist from Montreal, Canada, started writing about his theories of neural plasticity. Scientists and researchers from around the world were sharing theories and research as they developed an understanding of brain pasticity. This is how scientific revolutions happen over time.

As you read in Barbara's story, Mark Rosenzweig, an American research psychologist from the University of California, was one of the first scientists to observe brain plasticity in rats. Rats that were given an opportunity to play in an enriched environment full of ladders, obstacles, and running wheels had better brains. At the same time, in the early 1970s, Barbara was doing her university studies in Ontario.

Mark Rosenzweig and his colleagues helped the scientific world understand that the brain was not permanently fixed—that it was instead "plastic," or changeable. Their work helped to confirm the theories of William James, Santiago Ramon y Cajal, Jerzy Konorski, and Donald Hebb that indeed the brain was plastic. It also inspired Barbara to think that maybe her own brain was plastic and that she could try to improve her weak brain areas.

Remember, by the late 1970s, scientists had proven only that a rat brain was plastic. Thus, many people challenged the idea that the human brain was also plastic. An active debate was taking place in the scientific world.

Barbara was part of this new group of scientists and researchers. There were others as well, including Michael Merzenich from the University of California. He had seen brain plasticity in animals, and he wanted to know if humans could show the same ability to change their brains. With his colleagues, Merzenich created cognitive interventions to help people with a variety of brain disorders.

It took many years for neuroscientists to widely accept that the human brain is plastic, but today it is common knowledge. Norman Doidge, a Canadian psychiatrist and author who wrote the bestselling books The Brain That Changes Itself and The Brain's Way of Healing, has helped people understand the important implications of brain plasticity.

Today, teachers and parents realize that the brain is plastic. Research on reading disabilities has shown that the brain changes with different types of reading instruction. Brain-training exercises have shown that memory and attention can be improved in the brains of children with learning disabilities and attention problems. Still, some people continue to believe that learning disabilities are lifelong. It is important to remember that being a scientist sometimes requires courage and determination to challenge existing beliefs or ideas.

It is an exciting time to study how children and adults can improve brain functioning and also how we can bring this knowledge into schools across the world. This scientific revolution is going to help many children and adults with learning disabilities.

10 Amazing Brain Facts

1.

An adult brain weighs only 1.5 kilograms (3.3 pounds). That is about the weight of 10 bananas, or a bag of oranges or apples, or even the size of a smaller chihuahua. By the time you are 2 years old, your brain is 80% of the size it will be when you are an adult.

2.

Most people have 50,000 to 70,000 thoughts a day, or 35 to 48 thoughts per minute. Wow!

3.

Your brain is 75% water! This is a reminder to stay hydrated by drinking lots of water,especially on hot days or when you exercise. If you become dehydrated, your brain can have a harder time working properly.

4.

Your brain is still working when you are asleep. In fact, when you sleep, your brain is recovering from working hard during the day. This period of recovery helps your brain store memories (including the times tables you might have learned at school that day!) and be able to recall those memories the next day and further into the future.

5.

Your brain makes up only 2% to 4% of your body weight depending on your age. That's not much, considering your brain runs the show and controls everything you do during the day and night.

6.

The cerebrum contains between 85 billion and 100 billion neurons (also called brain cells) and 100 billion glial (support) cells. In comparison, the Milky Way is estimated to have anywhere from 100 to 400 billion stars.

7.

Those 100 billion neurons in your brain could make enough electricity to power a low-watt light bulb!

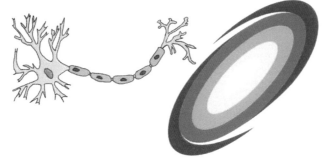

8.

Your brain makes new brain cells, or neurons, throughout your school years. That's right! Your brain is making new brain cells every minute of every day.

9.

The messages moving through the neural pathways in your brain can travel at speeds of up to 431 kilometers (268 miles) per hour. No land animal can run that fast! The cheetah is closest, reaching speeds of 120 kilometers (75 miles) per hour. A Formula One racing car can reach speeds of up to 386 kilometers (240 miles) per hour—still slower than your brain!

10.

You can survive with only half of your brain. Some people have up to half of their brain removed because of severe seizure disorders. This is called a *hemispherectomy*. They can still live a healthy and happy life with good cognitive functioning.

10 Ways to Keep Your Brain Healthy

1. Exercise

Do aerobic exercise to get more oxygen to the brain! This is exercise that stimulates the heart. Research has shown that aerobic exercise can increase brain size and improve your ability to figure things out and pay attention. Get out and exercise at least once a day for 30 minutes. You can: speed walk, hike, run, skateboard, play tag, jump rope, snowboard, bike, swim, cheerlead, do gymnastics, dance, cross-country ski, skate, and/or play sports such as tennis, soccer, and volleyball.

2. Get out into nature

Research shows that nature helps relax your brain when it is feeling worried or stressed. Blood pressure drops, and the front of the brain (called the *prefrontal cortex*) is shown to be calmer in nature. Get your parents to take your family camping or skating outdoors, or for a walk in a local park or forest. A visit to the beach is another option. You can even find nature to watch during a walk through a city neighborhood: sidewalk trees, potted plants, and hedges, and look out for city animals: dogs, cats, birds, squirrels, and racoons, to name a few.

3. Eat healthy foods

Do your best to avoid too much sugar or too much junk or fast food. Instead, try nuts, seeds, vegetables of different colors (for instance, spinach, carrots, broccoli, tomatoes, and mushrooms), fish, eggs, plain yogurt, berries, apples, oranges, and oatmeal, to name just some of the healthier food choices. Talk to your parents and your doctor about healthy eating habits.

4. Relax and get a good night's sleep

When you feel stressed out or worried, it affects your brain by increasing the stress hormone *cortisol*. Relaxing helps your brain by reducing the amount of cortisol. Too much cortisol in the brain, for long periods of time, can damage brain structure (neurons and their connections in the brain). You can relax by lying flat on your back on the floor or on your own bed and trying to let all your muscles go loose like cooked noodles. Or you can count slowly to 10 or 20 or 50 (as high as you need to go) or spend some time taking slow, deep breaths. A warm bath or shower can also help, as can listening to quiet music like classical music or nature sounds. Sometimes it can help if you remind yourself to think about things that make you happy or calm, such as being at the beach or curling up with a book or hugging your parents.

Getting a good night's sleep leads to better school performance and fewer behavior problems. Sleeping allows your brain to refresh itself for a new day and helps your memory system store information you learned the day before. Have a regular bedtime, even on Saturday and Sunday. Try some of the relaxing ideas noted above at least 30 minutes before you go to bed, such as having a warm bath or listening to relaxing music.

5. Learn new information and tasks

Learning new information is good for the brain. *Neuroplasticity* or brain change, occurs when your brain is presented with new knowledge and tasks that are mentally challenging and cause your brain to grow. You might want to join a group or club where you'll have to learn something new, such as how to play chess, how to memorize lines for a play, or how to use a compass or a sewing machine. New activities might be hard at the beginning, but over time your brain will develop the necessary *neural connections* (that's when your brain can increase in volume) for you to master the activity.

6. Speak other languages

Science has shown that learning a new language helps with memory and concentration, and even delays brain diseases like dementia or Alzheimer's (which you probably don't have to worry about yet, but it never hurts to start early!). Learning a second language can increase the size of your brain's language center (in the *superior temporal gyrus* area) and the hippocampus.

7. Play a musical instrument

Science is showing that when you learn to play music your brain begins to hear and process sounds that you could not before. Pretty awesome. As a bonus, this stimulation of the brain can lead to better school performance. How does this happen? The musical instrument could be stimulating the motor, auditory, organization, planning, and memory cortices. This stimulation would then provide a benefit to other learning activities, such as math, that also require these cortices.

8. Make friends

Form new friendships and keep your old friendships strong. Spending time with a friend can increase brain chemicals (such as serotonin) that calm you down and make you feel good. When you feel calm and happy it's easier to think things through carefully and make decisions more wisely. Friends make your brain healthier and stronger.

9. Avoid bad habits

Don't smoke, drink alcohol, or do drugs. Many research articles discuss the dangers of excessive drinking, drug use, and smoking on your brain (and on your body, too!). Stay brain healthy by avoiding them all.

10. Change your mindset

Carol Dweck, a professor at Stanford University in California, developed the term *growth mindset.* Growth mindset is the belief that your ability to learn, or your intelligence, is developed through hard work and dedication to learning. If you *believe* you can achieve success in a school subject by effort and determination, then most likely you *will* achieve that goal. Keep a growth mindset!

Glossary

Academic

A teacher or professor who works at a college or university. Most academics continue to study and do research in their field even after they graduate. *My uncle is an academic at the University of California, studying and teaching mathematics.*

Analogue clock

An analogue clock (or watch) has moving hands, and the minutes and hours are marked by the numbers 1 to 12. *The shorter hand on my analogue watch points to the hour.*

Auditory

If you describe something as auditory, it is related to hearing. *I need help with my auditory processing because I find it hard to follow classroom discussions.*

Axon, Nerve axon

A long, thread-like structure connected to a nerve cell that sends electrical impulses to other target cells. *Each nerve cell has one axon.*

Brain

The organ inside the head, made up of soft nervous tissue, that controls thoughts, memory, feelings and activity. *My brain allows me to learn how to make friends by understanding their feelings and emotions.*

Bullfight

A public event in an arena, seen in Spain, Portugal, and Latin America, in which a bullfighter (or matador) shows off their skill in avoiding the threat of being killed by a bull before killing it with a sword. *The movie The Matador showed just how dangerous it is to be involved in a bullfight. (Note: Because bullfighting is very dangerous for the matador, and considered by many to be cruel to the bulls, it has been stopped and even outlawed in many places).*

Cerebellum

In the back of the brain. Controls balance, movement, and muscles. *People who have a stroke in the cerebellum have difficulty standing up and maintaining their balance.*

Cerebral cortex

The outer layer of the cerebrum. It is responsible for thinking, language, and the creation of new ideas. *I use my cerebral cortex when I write a story in creative writing class.*

Cerebrum

The largest part of the brain. Divided into two halves. *The cerebrum makes up 85% of the brain's weight. My cerebrum is in the front of my skull.*

Character

A person's character is formed by the way they think, feel, and behave, or their overall personality. *Jess has a wonderful character, for she is kind and generous to others.*

Compensations

Finding ways to work around a learning difficulty by avoiding areas of weakness in learning, and/or by finding alternate methods that make use of your strengths. *My brother uses compensations (or compensation strategies) such as audio books when studying for tests.*

Concept

An idea conceived in the mind, or an understanding of something. *The concept of a car usually includes a vehicle with moving wheels.*

Connection

A relationship in which a person, thing, or idea is linked or associated with something else. *You must understand the connection between the position of the hands on a clock and the numbers they point to in order to tell time.*

Cortisol

A chemical substance (or hormone) often connected to the stress response of the body and brain. It plays an important role in helping the body respond to stress. *My family doctor wanted to test the <u>cortisol</u> level in my blood to make sure it was not too high and causing my body harm.*

Dendrite (means "branched like a tree")

The dendrites are the part of the neuron that receive stimulation so that a cell can become active. *The <u>dendrites</u> of a neuron cell can grow in complexity through stimulation.*

Despair

A complete loss of hope. *My friend was in complete <u>despair</u> after failing his math test.*

Determination

The will or drive to continue to try to do something even when it's difficult or may take a long time. *My friend Sam would study two hours a day, after a two-hour soccer practice, all week, for four weeks, to get an A on a math test. His <u>determination</u> was amazing.*

Digital clock

Shows the exact time only in numbers or digits, as opposed to an analogue clock where a more approximate time is displayed by rotating hands (often with a second, minute and hour hand) that point to the numbers. *The <u>digital clock</u> near my bed always reminds me to wake up at 6:00 a.m.*

Dyslexia

A type of learning disability that involves difficulty in acquiring and processing language. Children and adults with dyslexia struggle to read or interpret words, letters, and other symbols. *My brother has <u>dyslexia</u>. After much hard work, he learned to read when he was 15 years old.*

Educator

A person who teaches a skill or subject. *A second-grade teacher is an <u>educator</u>.*

Electrical engineer

A type of engineering (or building or designing) that deals with the uses of electricity. Often involves designing, testing, and supervising the development and manufacturing of electric motors, power generators, radar, and other communication systems. *The electrical engineer at my mother's company was very good at coming up with new ideas to solve customer problems.*

Emotion

A strong feeling (like anger, love, fear or joy) often connected with a physical reaction (yelling, hugging, crying or laughing). *I felt strong emotions when my parents brought home a new puppy.*

Enrich

To improve the quality of something by adding value to it. *I enriched the cookies I was baking by adding more chocolate chips.*

Frontal lobe

The largest of the four major lobes of the cerebral cortex. This part of the brain is used for decision making, planning, and thinking. *Alan was not able to work after his frontal lobe brain injury because he could not plan his schedule for the week.*

Functional magnetic resonance imaging (fMRI)

An fMRI measures brain activity by detecting changes in blood flow in the brain. When an area of the brain is in use, blood flow to that region increases. When a brain area is damaged there is less blood flow as it is not in use, and an fMRI will show this in the scan. *My cousin had an fMRI after his motorcycle accident to see whether his brain had been damaged.*

Functioning

Working or operating in a certain way. *Is my brain functioning the way it's supposed to when I try to read?*

Glial cells

Support cells that surround neurons and provide insulation. *There are many glial cells in the brain as there are neurons.*

Hemispherectomy

A surgical treatment for epilepsy. During the surgery one of the two hemispheres in the brain is removed, which, it is hoped, may stop or reduce the seizures. *My friend had a hemispherectomy because his doctor said it would reduce his uncontrollable seizures.*

Hippocampus

A region in the brain used for memories and connecting them to our emotions. *My hippocampus helps me remember things that have made me happy, like going to the waterpark last summer.*

Idea

A thought or collection of thoughts that are generated in the mind, often in relation to solving a problem, attaining a goal, or taking a new approach to something. *The pirate finally found the treasure after he got the idea to search under the abandoned lifeboat.*

Immune system

A system in the body that helps fight off infections and disease. *My immune system is strong and I did not get sick even though everyone else in my class did.*

Inventiveness

The same as creativity: being very good at thinking of original or new or unusual ideas. *Josh's inventiveness meant the kite he built was the most aerodynamic, and it won the contest.*

Kinesthetic perception

Also called "muscle memory", or your ability to be aware of your own movements when walking, eating, writing, or even brushing your teeth. *Barbara's kinesthetic perception was not very good when she was younger. She often bumped into things.*

Learning disability

A neurological disorder. Often associated with difficulty learning to read, write, and understand math. A learning disability may affect how a person absorbs, organizes, and retains verbal or nonverbal information. This also interferes with the ability to learn. *My friend has a <u>learning disability</u> in reading, so he is getting tutoring in phonics.*

Memory

Your brain's ability to store and recall facts or information it has learned. *I use my <u>memory</u> when I study for tests at school.*

Mental task

An activity that requires focus and thought. *I was given many <u>mental tasks</u> when the psychologist tested my IQ.*

Myelin water imaging (MWI)

A type of brain imaging that looks at myelin. Myelin is a soft, white, fatty material that covers nerve axons and serves as an electrical insulator that speeds up communication between cells. *The neuroscientist looked at my <u>MWI</u> and told me I had a healthy amount of myelin in my brain. This meant that my brain could perform tasks efficiently.*

Neural connection

Links between neurons. *There are trillions of <u>neural connections</u> in the brain.*

Neural pathways

These series of connected neurons allow signals to be sent from one brain region to another. *A healthy brain has strong <u>neural pathways</u>.*

Neural synapses

These series of connected neurons allow signals to be sent from on brain region to another. *<u>Neural synapses</u> are critical for proper brain functioning.*

Neuron

Neurons (also called "nerve cells") carry electrical messages from one part of the body to another. Neurons have parts called dendrites and axons that are used to communicate messages. *The brain is estimated to have 100 billion (100,000,000,000) neurons.*

Neuroplasticity

The process through which your brain's neural synapses and pathways can change and adapt. The brain has a remarkable ability to change, remodel, and reorganize itself when learning or adapting to new situations in life. *Children with learning disabilities will benefit from further research into neuroplasticity. Many of their learning challenges may not be lifelong if their brains can be molded to overcome their disabilities.*

Neuropsychologist

A person who studies the relationships among behavior, emotion, learning (also called "cognition"), and brain functioning. *I want to become a neuropsychologist so I can understand why people struggle to read and then help them discover whether their brain is functioning differently from an average reader's.*

Neuroscience

The study of the brain and nervous system. A neuroscientist works in this field. *Researchers in neuroscience and education are working together to develop a better understanding of how to help children with learning disabilities.*

Neurotransmitter

A chemical substance that helps send of transmit nerve impulses across a synapse. *A neurotransmitter is called a chemical messenger as it is sent by a neuron to communicate with other neurons.*

Nonverbal information

Information that is communicated without words. *If I would like my friend to help me with something, I communicate that with nonverbal information such as gesturing or holding my hands together like I am in prayer.*

Nutritionist

A person who studies how food and meals (nutrition) impact human health. *Because Barbara's mother was a trained <u>nutritionist</u>, she knew how important it was for her family to eat balanced meals that included protein, calcium, and lots of fruit and vegetables.*

Occipital lobe

One of the four major lobes of the cerebral cortex in humans. The visual processing center. *If your <u>occipital lobe</u> is damaged you may struggle to find your wallet, baseball hat, or even your shoes.*

Paradigm

A way of looking at some aspect of the world: a model of, or a way of viewing the world that is accepted by an individual or by society. *A recent <u>paradigm</u> in neuroscience features the idea that the brain can change itself, rather than being fixed or unalterable for life.*

Parietal lobe

One of the four major lobes of the cerebral cortex in humans. It plays an important role in your perception of body sensations or processing of sensory information, especially touch. *The <u>parietal lobe</u> is very important in helping you make sense of what you are holding in your hand.*

Parietal-temporal-occipital (PTO) association area

An area of the brain located in the cerebral cortex of the human brain. It is responsible for assembling auditory, visual, and touch/movement information. Because the parietal-temporal-occipital association area contains parts of three of the brain's lobes, it's able to process stimuli from each of them at the same time, which helps you comprehend the meaning of events and experiences. *Barbara was able to increase her understanding of the world by improving the <u>parietal-temporal-occipital association area</u> of her brain.*

Passion

A strong feeling of excitement or enthusiasm for something. *I was full of passion about my championship soccer game on Sunday.*

Paternal grandmother

Your paternal grandmothers if your father's mother. *Louie May was Barbara's father's mother, and thus her paternal grandmother. (Your maternal grandmother is your mother's mother. You also have a paternal and a maternal grandfather).*

Pathologist

An expert who studies or investigates diseases and illnesses. Someone who examines dead bodies. *The insightful pathologist figured out how the man had died.*

Persistence

Continuing to do something even if it is very difficult. *My sister knocked on my bedroom door with persistence until, after 15 minutes, I finally let her in.*

Philosopher

A person who studies ideas about the meaning of life or ideas about knowledge and truth. *The philosopher came up with an idea about why some people work so hard.*

Physicist

An expert in a science that focuses on all things that exist in the physical world, such as matter and energy. *Barbara's father was a trained physicist, allowing him to understand how matter and energy interact with each other.*

Pioneer

A person who explores or settles a new area or country. It can also mean a person who is the first to use or apply a new area of knowledge or new activity or method. *Barbara Arrowsmith-Young is a pioneer in the fields of education and neuroscience.*

Plasticity

The quality of or capacity for being molded or altered—changed. *The brain has remarkable plasticity.*

Pneumonia

A lung inflammation caused by an infection, often resulting in a fever and coughing, and making it difficult to breathe. *My grandfather for pneumonia when he was in Alaska and needed to take medication to reduce his fever.*

Psychiatry

The science of treating people who have emotional, behavioral, and mental disorders like anxiety, depression and schizophrenia. *Tim is interested in practicing psychiatry so he can help people with depression.*

Psychology

The scientific study of the human mind and its functions or behavior. *Sarah is interested in studying psychology at university because she wants to become an expert in figuring out why people behave the way they do.*

Quantitative electroencephalography (qEEG)

This is also called "brain mapping". It is a non-invasive (which means no instruments or devices are put into the body) way to measure brain functioning and connectivity. This technique of measuring brain activity provides highly precise measurements. *The study of how the Arrowsmith Program improved the brain functioning of individuals with traumatic brain injury used quantitative electroencephalography (qEEG) to highlight brain change.*

Reasoning

The process of thinking about facts in order to make a decision or judgement, or to solve a problem. *Mary used reasoning to come up with an answer for why Cecilia did not show up for school even though last night Cecilia had said she was feeling fine.*

Relationship

The way in which two or more concepts, objects, or people are connected. *Barbara had to work hard to understand the <u>relationship</u> between groups of numbers so that she could do her math assignments.*

Researcher

A person who does academic or scientific studies. *Dr. Greg Rose is a <u>researcher</u> who is studying the Arrowsmith Program to observe what changes are occurring in the brain.*

Resilience

The ability to recover quickly from a difficulty or tragedy. *Sam showed amazing <u>resilience</u> after breaking his leg in a snowboarding accident. He is dealing well with the emotional ups and downs of recovering from such an accident.*

Revolution, revolutionary

A sudden, complete, or a drastic change, often in thought, or in political situations. *Barbara's belief that the brain can change itself and that children with learning disabilities can therefore improve their cognitive functioning was <u>revolutionary</u>.*

Serotonin

A chemical produced in the brain that can control how you feel. *The level or amount of <u>serotonin</u> in your brain will affect your mood or state of mind, influencing whether you are happy or calm.*

Stimulate

To encourage or cause something to grow, develop, or become active. *I hoped that my science course would <u>stimulate</u> a love for learning in my students.*

Spatial reasoning

The ability to think of objects in two or three dimensions and to be able to to rotate them in your mind and determine what their position would be after they have been moved. *Being able to take a motor apart and later remember how it all fits back together again requires good <u>spatial reasoning</u>.*

Special education

A carefully designed way of teaching children who struggle with learning. Special education teachers are trained to work with unique types of learning difficulties such as autism, learning disabilities, and ADHD. They may also work with children who have physical handicaps such as head injuries and cerebral palsy. *My school has special education classrooms for students who need extra support in learning.*

Strategy

A careful plan or method for achieving a particular goal. *I came up with a strategy to get out of doing my chores on weekends.*

Superior temporal gyrus

The site of the auditory association cortex, critical for processing sounds. *Research shows that the superior temporal gyrus can distinguish between the tiniest speech details.*

Temporal lobe

One of the four major lobes in the cerebral cortex, involved in processing what we hear. *When Jeff's temporal lobe was injured he couldn't hear very well and struggled to understand what people were saying to him.*

Traumatic brain injury

A disruption of brain functioning caused by a blow, jolt, or bump to the head, or penetrating head injury (an object going into the brain). *The soldier suffered a traumatic brain injury when a bullet was lodged in his cerebrum.*

Trustee

A person who oversees the administrative tasks of a school, company, or institution. *Barbara's mother was a school trustee in Peterborough. She spent a lot of time as a trustee dealing with new school initiatives brought forward by the public.*

University

A place where people go to learn and study after high school. Degrees are given in special fields of study and research is performed. *My mother went to <u>university</u> after high school and earned a psychology degree. Now she works as a counselor in Boston helping students transition from high school to college.*

Verbal information

Facts, details, or figures that are communicated through words, whether the words are spoken aloud or read silently on paper or on-screen. *Isabella enjoys using <u>verbal information</u>, such as talks on YouTube, for understanding ideas rather than just thinking in visual images.*

Bibliography and Web Resources

BOOKS

Arrowsmith-Young, Barbara. *The Woman Who Changed Her Brain: How I Left My Learning Disability Behind and Other Stories Of Cognitive Transformation.* New York: Simon & Schuster, 2012.

Doidge, Norman. *The Brain That Changes Itself: Stories of Personal Triumph from the Frontiers of Brain Science.* New York: Penguin Group, 2007.

Doidge, Norman. *The Brain's Way of Healing: Remarkable Discoveries and Recoveries from the Frontiers of Neuroplasticity.* New York: Penguin Group, 2015.

Eaton, Howard. *Brain school: Stories of Children with Learning Disabilities and Attention Disorders Who Changed Their Lives by Improving Their Cognitive Functioning.* Vancouver: Glia Press, 2011.

Fernandez, Alvaro. *The Sharpbrains Guide to Brain Fitness: How to Optimize Brain Health and Performance at Any Age.* Charleston, SC: Sharpbrains, Inc., 2013.

Kuhn, Thomas. *The Structure of Scientific Revolutions.* Chicago: University of Chicago Press, 2012. (Originally published in 1962).

Luria, A.R. *The Man with a Shattered World: The History of a Brain Wound.* New York: Basic Books, Inc., 1972.

WEBSITES

Kid Friendly

Neuroscience for Kids: University of Washington. Managed by Eric H. Chudler, Ph.D., and previously assisted by a Science Education Partnership Award (R25RR12312) from the National Center for Research Resources (NCRR).
http://faculty.washington.edu/chudler/neurok.html

Kids Health- Nemours Foundation's Center for Children's Health Media: KidsHealth is a popular site on the web for knowledge about behavior, health, and development from birth through the teen years.
http://kidshealth.org/en/kids/brain.html

Brains On! A Podcast for Kids & Curious Adults. Funded in part by the National Science Foundation.
http://www.brainson.org/

Brainfacts.org. A public information initiative of the Kavli Foundation, the Gatsby Charitable Foundation, and the Society for Neuroscience- global nonprofit organizations focused on advancing brain research.
http://www.brainfacts.org/core-concepts/your-complex-brain

Easy Science for Kids. Free online resource for teachers, parents, tutors, and educators and where children can have fun learning all about science through extensive articles, free science worksheets, and downloadable science activity sheets, education interactive science quizzes, coloring-in activities, science experiment tips and ideas, and large collection of the best science videos.
http://easyscienceforkids.com/all-about-your-amazing-brain/

For educators and Parents

Sharpbrains. An independent market research firm and brain trust monitoring health and performance applications of brain science.
https://sharpbrains.com/

The Dana Foundation. A private philanthropic organization centered in New York devoted to advancing brain research and to informing the public in an accountable manner about the potential of that research.
http://www.dana.org/

The Human Brain Project. A 10-year scientific research project that is directed at building a collaborative ICT-based scientific research infrastructure to let researchers across Europe to further knowledge in the fields of neuroscience, computing, and brain-related medicine.
https://www.humanbrainproject.eu/en/

Creston, B.C. c. 1920
Arrowsmith Ranch

1960 Barbara age 9

1965 — Barbara and Star
age 14

1966 Grade 10 age 15

Queen Mary in
Peterborough, ON.

Barbara with Mother and Brothers
1956 age 5

Winter 1952 - Louie May and Barbara (1 year old)

1980 Barbara with her Parents age 28

Arrowsmith School, Toronto, Ontario

2000 - Barbara at her desk

1954 - Barbara 3 yrs. old and brother Donald 1 yr. old

Barbara and Donald February 2018, Toronto, ON

ABOUT THE AUTHOR

Howard Eaton was seven years old when he was diagnosed with severe dyslexia. He dropped out of school in grade five and attended a private school for children with dyslexia, the Kildonan School. After learning to read, write, and spell, he went on to university to earn a Bachelor of Arts degree in psychology at the University of British Columbia, and a master's degree in special education at Boston University. He has started five schools that help children and adults with learning disabilities. You can learn more about his work at **www.howardeaton.com**.

ABOUT THE ILLUSTRATOR

Kezzia Crossley resides in Vancouver, British Columbia, Canada. She has an immense passion for conceptualizing characters and bringing stories to life. You can see more of her work at **www.kezziacrossley.ca**.